ROCK STARS

CRYSTALS AND GEMSTONES

By Chris and Helen Pellant

Gareth Stevens
Publishing

Please visit our web site at **www.garethstevens.com**. For a free catalog describing Gareth Stevens Publishing's list of high-quality books, call 1-800-542-2595 (USA) or 1-800-387-3178 (Canada). Gareth Stevens Publishing's fax: 1-877-542-2596

Library of Congress Cataloging-in-Publication Data

Pellant, Chris.
    Crystals and gemstones / Chris and Helen Pellant. — U.S. ed.
       p. cm. — (Rock stars)
    Includes index.
    ISBN-10: 0-8368-9222-4   ISBN-13: 978-0-8368-9222-2 (lib. bdg.)
    1. Crystals—Juvenile literature. 2. Crystal growth—Juvenile literature. 3. Mineralogy—Juvenile literature. 4. Precious stones—Juvenile literature. I. Pellant, Helen. II. Title.
    QD906.3.P45   2009
    548—dc22   2008016120

This North American edition first published in 2009 by
Gareth Stevens Publishing
A Weekly Reader® Company
1 Reader's Digest Road
Pleasantville, NY 10570-7000 USA

This U.S. edition copyright © 2009 by Gareth Stevens, Inc. Original edition copyright © 2008 by ticktock Media Ltd. First published in Great Britain in 2008 by ticktock Media Ltd., 2 Orchard Business Centre, North Farm Road, Tunbridge Wells, Kent, TN2 3XF.

For ticktock:
Project Editor: Julia Adams   Project Designer: Emma Randall
Picture Researcher: Lizzie Knowles   With thanks to Terry Jennings, Graham Rich, Joe Harris

For Gareth Stevens:
Senior Managing Editor: Lisa M. Herrington   Creative Director: Lisa Donovan
Senior Editor: Barbara Bakowski   Electronic Production Manager: Paul Bodley

Picture credits (t = top; b = bottom; c = center; l = left; r = right):
age fotostock/SuperStock: 3l, 21tr. iStock: 3E, 5t, 9t, 10cl, 12tl, 12cr x2, 12cl, 13cr, 22t, 23tr, 23cl. Ben Mangor/SuperStock: 15t. North Wind Picture Archives/Alamy: 14b. Jack Novak/SuperStock: 23bl. Chris & Helen Pellant: 3B, 6t, 6c, 6b, 7t, 8bl x2, 9c, 9b, 11tr, 16 all, 17l x3, 18 all, 19l x3, 20 all, 21l x3. Photodisc/Photolibrary: 7br. Pool Photograph/Corbis: 22c. Scientifica/Visuals Unlimited/Alamy: 11r. Shutterstock: 1, 2, 3A, C, D, F, G, H, J, K, L, 4tl, 4bl, 4br, 5bl, 5bc, 5br, 7c, 7bl, 8tl, 10tl, 10cr, 10bl, 10br, 11l x3, 12bl x2, 12br, 13tl, 13tr, 13cl, 13bl, 13br, 14tl, 14cl, 14cr, 15c all, 17tr, 17br x2, 19tr, 19br, 21br x2, 23tl, 25tl. Javier Trueba/MSF/Science Photo Library: 22ft. Roland Weihrauch/dpa/Corbis: 22b. Wikipedia: 23cr.

Every effort has been made to trace copyright holders, and we apologize in advance for any omissions. We would be pleased to insert the appropriate acknowledgments in any subsequent edition of this publication.

Printed in the United States of America

1 2 3 4 5 6 7 8 9 10 09 08

Contents

Words that appear in **bold** are explained in the glossary.

What Are Crystals?

Jewels are among the most prized objects in the world. Most jewels are natural substances that formed as **crystals**. Crystals have flat sides, angled edges, and sharp corners. They can be many different sizes, colors, and shapes.

You can find crystals in many places. Some crystals form in caves deep underground. Others form inside stones or at the seashore.

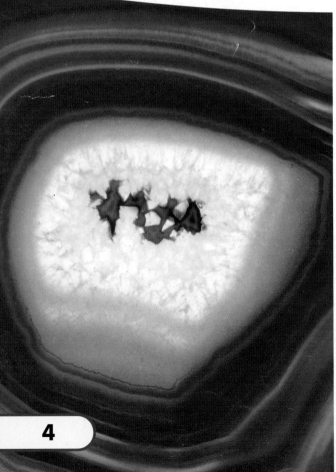

Some crystals are brightly colored. These are quartz crystals.

Some crystals are shiny and metallic. This is pyrite.

It's a Fact!
Naturally formed ice is a kind of crystal. When ice melts and turns into liquid water, it is no longer a crystal.

Icicles on a branch

Crystals are all around us. Foods such as salt and sugar are made up of many small crystals. We even have crystals in our bodies! Our bones are made of millions of tiny crystals.

People use crystals to make things. For example, crystals are used in clocks and video game consoles. Sometimes we shape crystals in beautiful ways. Then they are called **gemstones**.

How Do Crystals Form?

Minerals are solid substances that occur naturally in Earth. All rocks are made up of minerals. Sometimes minerals form as crystals.

Crystals in Rocks

Most of Earth's crystals were formed millions of years ago. Crystals form when **molten rock** from inside Earth cools and hardens. If the molten rock cools quickly, the crystals in it are tiny. If the rock cools slowly, the crystals may be quite large. Rock that forms in this way is called **igneous rock**.

Granite is an igneous rock.

Sandstone is a sedimentary rock.

Rocks can be worn down by wind, heat, cold, and moving ice or water. The rocks break down into small grains called sediment. Sediment can contain tiny pieces of crystal. Sometimes sediment forms layers. The layers are squeezed together. They form **sedimentary rock**.

Gneiss is a metamorphic rock.

Deep within Earth, there is a lot of heat and pressure. **Metamorphic rock** forms when heat, pressure, or both cause changes in igneous or sedimentary rock. Granite can change to form gneiss (pronounced "nice"). When rocks change, the crystals in them change, too. Compare the patterns in the granite and gneiss shown here.

Surface Crystals

Crystals can form on the surface of Earth. This happens in many different ways.

Water that cools naturally turns into ice crystals.

*Sometimes molten rock bursts to the surface through a **volcano**. Then it cools and forms crystals.*

*When seawater **evaporates**, salt crystals form.*

Crystal Shapes

Crystals can form in many different shapes. They can have many surfaces or just a few. The surfaces can be different shapes and may be joined in different ways, too.

The surfaces of crystals are called **faces**. When the faces of a crystal join, they can make a shape that looks the same from all sides. Such crystals are **symmetric**.

Pyrite forms in **cube >>** shapes. Each crystal has six square faces.

Natural rock base

<< Fluorite crystals have eight faces. Each face is the shape of a triangle. The crystal looks like two pyramids stuck together.

Mica is one of >> the minerals that make up granite. Mica forms in flat, thin crystals.

Gypsum crystals >> are thin and long. They look like needles.

Hematite has a >> rounded bubble shape. The bubbles are formed by tiny crystals. The crystals are so small, they cannot be seen with the naked eye.

Which Crystal?

There are many different ways of identifying a crystal. Besides shape, you can look at its color and test its hardness.

Colorful Crystals

Crystals come in many colors and shades. Some crystals have more than one color.

Citrine is a combination of white and bright yellow. It is often used in jewelry.

Rose quartz gets its name from its light pink color.

Topaz usually has a soft golden color. When it has a hint of pink, it is called imperial topaz.

Malachite is a very deep green. Long ago, it was used to make paint.

You can use the Crystal Collector section on pages 16–21 to find out more about the colors of crystals.

Crystal Hardness

We use a scale from 1 to 10 to test the hardness of crystals. Crystals that have a measurement of 10 are the hardest. The crystals that are higher on the scale can scratch the crystals that are lower on the scale.

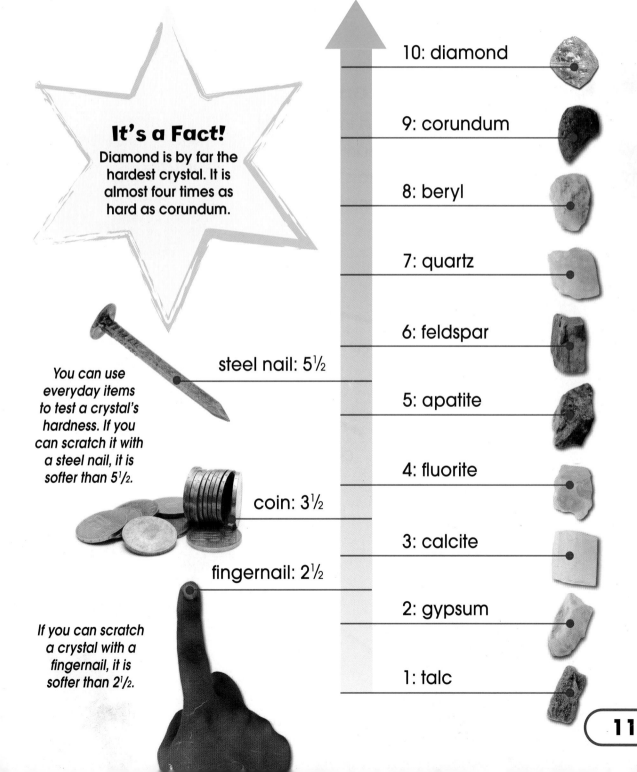

It's a Fact!
Diamond is by far the hardest crystal. It is almost four times as hard as corundum.

10: diamond

9: corundum

8: beryl

7: quartz

6: feldspar

steel nail: 5½

You can use everyday items to test a crystal's hardness. If you can scratch it with a steel nail, it is softer than 5½.

5: apatite

4: fluorite

coin: 3½

3: calcite

fingernail: 2½

2: gypsum

If you can scratch a crystal with a fingernail, it is softer than 2½.

1: talc

11

What Are Gemstones?

A gemstone is a mineral or crystal that has been cut and polished. It may be a sparkling diamond or a shimmering pearl.

From Crystal to Gemstone

Crystals can be cut and polished in a special way to make them shine and sparkle. Many gemstones are made from crystals that are very rare. That is why a lot of gemstones are very expensive.

Orpiment is cut and polished to make rubies.

Cut and polished corundum is called sapphire.

Emeralds are made from beryl crystals.

12

Organic Gemstones

Some gemstones are made of materials from animals or plants. Those gemstones are **organic**. Unlike crystals, they cannot be tested for hardness.

Resin

Amber

Amber

Amber is made of tree **resin**. Resin seeps out of the bark of trees and slowly hardens. Over millions of years, it turns into amber.

Coral

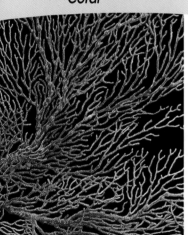

Coral beads

Coral

Coral is a hard material that forms in tree-like shapes. It is made by ocean creatures called **coral polyps**. Areas on the seabed that are covered in coral are called coral reefs.

Oyster with pearls

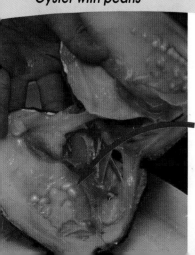

Pearl necklace

Pearl

Sometimes sand becomes trapped inside the shell of an oyster. The animal starts to coat the sand grain with shiny white crystals. The crystals build up in layers and form a pearl!

How We Use Gemstones

For centuries, gemstones have been important in many cultures. Gemstones can be a sign of power and wealth. Some people believe certain gemstones bring good luck.

Healing Powers

Ancient Egyptians believed that colored gemstones could heal people. Today, some people still practice this type of healing. They believe that placing crystals and gemstones on the body can help cure illnesses.

Good Hunting

Native Americans have been making objects from turquoise for 3,000 years. The stone has a special meaning for each native group. The Pueblo believe that attaching a piece of turquoise to a gun or a bow will give a hunter perfect aim.

A Pueblo ceremonial dance

Royal Gem

Diamond is the hardest and most precious gemstone. For centuries, it has been a symbol of wealth. Diamonds are often used in crowns and in fine jewelry.

TURQUOISE
December

GARNET
January

AMETHYST
February

AQUAMARINE
March

TOPAZ
November

Birthstones

Many countries have a tradition of birthstones. Each gemstone represents a certain month of the year. Many people wear the gemstone of their birth month. What is your birthstone?

DIAMOND
April

OPAL
October

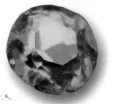

EMERALD
May

SAPPHIRE
September

PERIDOT
August

RUBY
July

PEARL
June

Crystal Collector

Augite

COLOR: black, dark green
FOUND: in igneous rock
HARDNESS: 6

Calcite

COLOR: white, pink, gray
FOUND: in sedimentary rock, **mineral veins**
HARDNESS: 3

Gypsum

COLOR: white, pink, green, brown
FOUND: in sedimentary rock
HARDNESS: 2

Halite (Rock Salt)

COLOR: pink, brown
FOUND: in sedimentary rock
HARDNESS: 2

Mica

COLOR: black, silvery white
FOUND: in igneous and metamorphic rock
HARDNESS: 2½

Milky Quartz

COLOR: white
FOUND: in mineral veins, igneous rock
HARDNESS: 7

Feldspar

COLOR: white, pink, bluish
FOUND: in igneous and metamorphic rock
HARDNESS: 6

Hornblende

COLOR: black, dark green
FOUND: in igneous rock
HARDNESS: 6

Tourmaline

COLOR: green, pink, black, blue
FOUND: in igneous rock
HARDNESS: 7

Finding Crystals

You can find crystals in many places. Rocks are made up of minerals, which sometimes form as crystals. When you go looking for crystals, you will need a kit of tools.

- a strong backpack for your tools and crystals

- newspaper or air-filled packing wrap to protect your crystals

- a rock hammer for breaking up loose rocks

- a magnifying glass to see close-up details

- goggles to protect your eyes from rock splinters

- a notebook and a pen for writing details about the crystals you collect

Crystal Collector

Gemstones

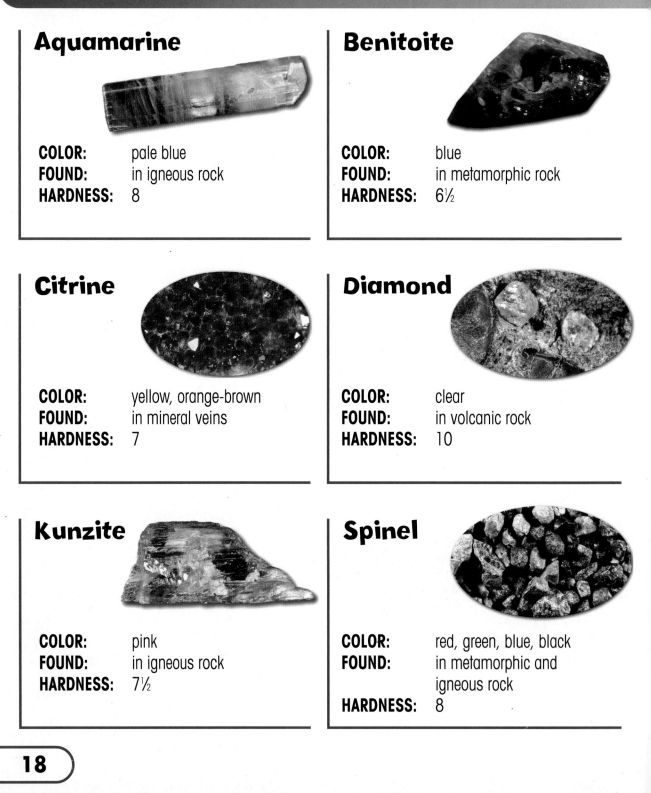

Aquamarine

COLOR:	pale blue
FOUND:	in igneous rock
HARDNESS:	8

Benitoite

COLOR:	blue
FOUND:	in metamorphic rock
HARDNESS:	6½

Citrine

COLOR:	yellow, orange-brown
FOUND:	in mineral veins
HARDNESS:	7

Diamond

COLOR:	clear
FOUND:	in volcanic rock
HARDNESS:	10

Kunzite

COLOR:	pink
FOUND:	in igneous rock
HARDNESS:	7½

Spinel

COLOR:	red, green, blue, black
FOUND:	in metamorphic and igneous rock
HARDNESS:	8

Cairngorm

COLOR: smoky brown
FOUND: in mineral veins, igneous rock
HARDNESS: 7

Emerald

COLOR: green
FOUND: in igneous rock
HARDNESS: 8

Zircon

COLOR: red, brown, yellow, green, gray
FOUND: in igneous rock
HARDNESS: 8

Collecting Gemstones

You can easily start a gemstone collection without spending a lot of money. Here are some tips.

- You may be able to buy gems at a local gem shop. You can also get advice on collecting gemstones.

- Mineral dealers sell crystals and gemstones. Many dealers have web sites.

- Join a local club for mineralogists or gemologists (people who specialize in minerals or gems). Other collectors may give you useful advice.

- Visit mineral shows and fairs.

Crystal Collector

More gemstones

Amber

COLOR: orange, brown
FOUND: in sedimentary rock
HARDNESS: cannot be tested (organic)

Azurite

COLOR: blue
FOUND: in mineral veins
HARDNESS: 4

Hematite

COLOR: red, brown, black
FOUND: in mineral veins, sedimentary rock
HARDNESS: 6

Jasper

COLOR: red
FOUND: in mineral veins, igneous rock
HARDNESS: 7

Lazurite

COLOR: blue
FOUND: in limestone
HARDNESS: 5½

Rhodochrosite

COLOR: pink, red
FOUND: in mineral veins
HARDNESS: 4

Blue John

COLOR: bands of blue and white
FOUND: in veins in limestone, a sedimentary rock
HARDNESS: 4

Jet

COLOR: black
FOUND: in sedimentary rock
HARDNESS: cannot be tested (organic)

Turquoise

COLOR: blue
FOUND: in sedimentary and igneous rock
HARDNESS: 5

Making Displays

Crystals and gemstones are ideal for display. These materials are delicate, however. Keep them away from dust and liquids. The less you handle your crystals, the better.

Here are some more hints for creating your display.

- Gently clean your samples with a soft paintbrush.

- Make card trays for your samples. For each section, write a label with the name of the crystal or gemstone.

- Leave crystals in their natural rock base to prevent damage.

- Display your most valuable samples behind glass.

Record Breakers

Biggest Crystals

To date, the largest natural crystals have been found in northern Mexico. These gypsum crystals are about 36 feet (11 meters) long! They formed in caves over millions of years.

Rarest Crystal

The rarest crystal is probably the diamond. Most diamonds are buried deep beneath Earth's surface. Miners must move tons of rock to get just one small diamond!

Oldest Large Cut Diamond

The oldest-known cut diamond is the Koh-i-Noor ("mountain of light"). Experts say it was found in India about 5,000 years ago. It is now part of the British crown jewels.

Room of Wonders

The Amber Room, in a palace in Russia, was made of several tons of amber. It took 10 years to build. The room was later destroyed in a war. A replica, or copy, was finished in 2003 in St. Petersburg.

Did You Know?

The Statue of Liberty in New York is made of copper. Its green color comes from atacamite crystals. They form when copper reacts with oxygen.

In the Middle Ages (about A.D. 500 to 1450), ladies sometimes gave rubies to their knights as tokens of love.

Thin pieces of sharpened diamond are used as knife blades in surgery. Diamond knives make smooth, exact cuts.

Some gems are cut so that they reflect a narrow band of light. This effect makes them look like cats' eyes.

Quartz crystals are used in many electronic devices, such as computers, TVs, and cell phones.

The Hope diamond is the largest and most perfect blue diamond. It is kept at the Smithsonian Institution in Washington, D.C.

For thousands of years, people have tried to tell the future using crystal balls. Usually, these crystal balls are made of quartz.

Gemstones are measured in carats. Most diamonds are smaller than 1 carat. The Hope diamond weighs 45.52 carats!

Pearls can come in many different colors: white, pink, gray. Some pearls are even black!

Glossary

coral polyps sea animals that attach to one another to create underwater rocky formations called coral reefs

crystals solid mineral forms with a regular shape and flat surfaces

cube a solid shape with six square sides

evaporates turns from a liquid into a gas. Water evaporates when it turns into water vapor.

faces naturally formed flat surfaces of a crystal

gemstones minerals that can be cut and polished for use in jewelry

igneous rock rock formed by the hardening of molten material from deep within Earth

metamorphic rock rock formed when heat, pressure, or both cause changes in rock minerals

minerals naturally formed materials that make up rocks. Many minerals form as crystals.

mineral veins thin masses of minerals that form between rock layers or in cracks in rocks

molten rock rock that is extremely hot and that flows like a liquid

organic having to do with living matter, such as animals and plants

resin a sticky yellow or brown material made by plants such as fir and pine trees

sedimentary rock rock that is formed when small bits of other rocks build up in layers and are squeezed together

symmetric balanced on either side of a dividing line or around a center

volcano a hole in Earth's crust through which molten rock bursts to the surface

Index